T0113812

HURT
&
HURT

Helping those who have experienced hurt and need healing

Experiencing & Overcoming HURT

Betty N. Waggoner

authorHOUSE®

Steps to Overcoming Hurt

H- Healing

U- Understanding

R- Restore

T- Trust

&

H- Hope and Help

U- Unity and
   Unconditional love

R- Respect

T- Teach and Transform

AuthorHouse™
1663 Liberty Drive
Bloomington, IN 47403
www.authorhouse.com
Phone: 1 (800) 839-8640

Published by AuthorHouse   08/03/2016

ISBN: 978-1-5246-1775-2 (sc)
ISBN: 978-1-5246-1774-5 (e)

Library of Congress Control Number: 2016911146

Print information available on the last page.

All Scriptures quotations are taken from the Holy Bible, New International Version;NIV; NKJV; and Message Bible

About the Book

This book is to help men, women, boys and girls of different races, ethnicities, religions, ages and backgrounds overcome hurt they have experienced in their lives. Hurt can be experienced in several different forms and can cause individuals to become distant, depressed and out of touch with their feelings.

Oftentimes in life many people will experience some form of hurt and may not know how to get through it on their own. I pray this book will be a devotional, motivational and inspirational guide to help others heal from their past, current and future distress.

This book will teach individuals how to forgive, love, trust, hope again and experience a divine healing in life so one can feel complete again. Healing can occur regardless of one's faith, religion or belief.

Contents

Hurt

Hurt is a psychological block of the human mind and heart that is caused by traumatic event in one's life. Hurt can be experienced through sickness in the body, unkind words, failed relationships, the death of a loved one, and the feeling of abandonment. Experiencing hurt can cause an individual to feel stagnant in life. Hurt can be shallow or deep and harder for a person to forgive or move on with their life. When a person experiences a situation they cannot function properly. For example when a record or CD is playing and gets damaged or scratched, the song will skip or stop playing. The song is now interrupted and cannot move forward until you remove the cd and examine it and find the problem. It has to go through a cleaning or healing process in order for the record to continue playing. Now you have the option of moving ahead to the next song or replaying the song with no interruptions. When people experience a form of grief or emotional distress the pain felt supersedes all the positive things in that person's life. It's like the mind continually replays the event that caused the pain or hurt. It is important to remember the example of the skipping record and how it simply needed to be cleaned.

The Heart

The heart is a sensitive yet powerful organ of the human body. When a person becomes wounded it affects their heart emotionally, mentally and physically. The human heart is what allows us to feel different emotions. It helps one to understand the feelings we feel like if we are happy, sad, or wounded. When family, friends, spouses betray or speak unkind words about us this can create a great deal of hurt when tragedies occur in life it also causes a great deal of pain. Sometimes we can cause our own hurt by making the wrong choices in life. Everyone feels hurt in different ways we all cope with it in different ways. If left untreated, the hurt one feels in life will take a toll on their heart and body.

The feelings of being hurt can go straight to a person's nerves and cause a person not eat, sleep or believe. It causes one to act out of character, to lose their faith. However hurt is not the only thing that we can feel in our heart. Joy, peace, and forgiveness come from the heart. God heals the brokenhearted and can bind up their wounds (Psalms 147:3 KJV). The lord is close to the broken hearted and saves those who are crushed in their spirit (Psalms 34:18 New International Version).

The heart is a masterpiece that God made and formed with his hands. He gave man the skills and knowledge to treat the heart when it is not emotionally or physically functioning properly due to situations that have caused tremendous pain or hurt.

Relationships

Webster dictionary defines relationship as the way in which two or more people are connected. Relationships are one of the most common ways for people to experience some form of hurt. In romantic relationships the most common form of hurt is due to infidelity on either the husband or wife behalf. Hurt can be caused by lack of communication, disrespect, and not spending enough quality time with one another due to work, children and family. Relationships needs to be nurtured and protected it takes a lot of work, prayer, patience and love to overcome hurt from a significant other or from someone you have developed a deep relationship with.

Good relationships should display patience, understanding, kindness, love, laughter, forgiveness, honesty and loyalty, everyone involved should have a certain degree of respect for one another and their feelings, opinions and beliefs.

Things that can help people overcome hurt in a relationship could be creating a date night, attending counseling, praying together, listening to one another without interruptions, showing affection to one another and taking the time to express when someone has offended you. Often times one may not know they have caused you hurt until you bring it to their attention and when you discuss it with the person like two adults you later find it was not their intention to cause you pain. There is no perfect relationship, every relationship will experience good and bad times it is how hard you work at fixing it that pays off in the long run.

"Again I say to you that if two of you agree on earth concerning anything that they ask, it will be done for them by My Father in heaven. For where two or three are gathered together in My name, I am there in the midst of them." (Matthew 18:19–20, NKJV).

Church Folks

Church used to be a place where people could go, when their hearts were wounded and needed a place to rest and worship God. Today some Church folks cause hurt from the pulpit to the sanctuary, from the sanctuary to behind closed doors leaving some people hurt and in distress and not wanting anything to do with religion or church.

Today church has turned into a fashion show, a joke and not a place where one can go to be delivered. There seems to be no unity and not enough love amongst the church goers and the church leaders. Today many people attend church to socialize, find men or women and have no real need of changing or worshiping God. In some churches today sexual crimes, financial crimes, adultery and other ungodly acts are all occurring behind closed doors. Leaving many people confused and upset with God and not knowing the difference between god and the enemy. Some church leaders care more about their title, making money, who has the largest church, the most members and living the good life, than saving souls. Leaving people to deal with their hurt on their own often time causing them to backslide and go back into the world. The Bible states, *"For the Son of man is come to save that which was lost."* (Matthew 18:11-14 KJV)

This is not to say all churches and church leaders are corrupt or not of God this is simply saying that we all have sinned and fall short of Gods glory. But what we can do is repent to those we have hurt, love one another free of judgment and seek to be more like God. Remember where there is unity there is love.

Love is patient and kind; love does not envy or boast; it is not arrogant or rude. It does not insist on its own way; it is not irritable or resentful; it does not rejoice at wrongdoing, but rejoices with the truth. Love bears all things, believes all things, hopes all things, and endures all things. Love never fails. (1 Corinthians 13:4-8 ESV)

Forgiveness

For many people forgiveness can sometimes be a hard thing to do. The bible teaches us that forgiveness is the most powerful tool we can utilize as Christians. When we hold on to hurt, it can cause sickness in the body, confusion, anger and make one stagnant in life. The true healing occurs when we forgive the people who have caused us the most pain in life. Letting go of hurt allows for personal growth. The following are scriptures I found to be helpful when dealing with hurt and forgiveness.

1 John 1:9 (NIV) If we confess our sins, he is faithful and just and will forgive us our sins and purify us from all unrighteousness.

Acts 3:19 (NIV) Repent, then, and turn to God, so that your sins may be wiped out, that times of refreshing may come from the Lord.

Ephesians 1:7 (NIV) In him we have redemption through his blood, the forgiveness of sins, in accordance with the riches of God's grace.

Daniels 9:9 (NIV) The Lord our God is merciful and forgiving, even though we have rebelled against him.

Family

Family can cause hurt and distress in many ways. Family can hurt you quicker and deeper than strangers. It is the people closest to us that have the power to hurt you the most. Some family carries bitterness, jealousy and hatred and can never get along or have unity leaving the family in shambles from generation to generation. Some members are jealous and cause confusion within the family by lying.

In some family there are mean spirited aunts, uncles, cousins, sisters and brothers and you would rather hide under the house with the chickens to feel safe, because you know under the house they will not be able to hurt or harm you. You would never imagine the level of hurt that could come from being hurt by your "family". You never think that it would be your family who lie, cheat, steal, and talk bad about you behind you back. It's even sadder when you have family members who do not consider you their family based on all the lies told by another family member. All you can do is Pray because life stops for no one. Just Know that "God heals the brokenhearted, and binds up their wounds (Psalms 147:3 NIV).

Know that at some point it is okay to walk away from family and leave them in the hands of God. You do not have to subject yourself to such pain simply because you all share the same blood. You can learn to love them from a distance. What is important is that you learn to love yourself and release bitterness, anger and malice thoughts against your family members that has caused you hurt (Matthew 18; 22 ESV).

In some families children can also experience hurt when there is an absence parents or maybe both parents are not in the home and the child is being raised by a family member or has been given up for adoption or the child never met one of their parent it can create a sense of rejection and abandonment. Children are innocent and do not deserve to be hurt by the choices their parents make in life. Sometimes God can keep people out of your life for a reason and have them appear at a divine time. God has a reason for everything we experience in life, our experiences throughout life can help make us stronger wiser and better. When we reach a place of forgiveness and self-empowerment we begin to understand why we had to go through all the hurt and pain. Hurt is something that crosses all denominations, religions, races, ethnicities and genders. It does not discriminate, it has no bias. Hurt is something that can be defeated.

H—Healing

God heals the broken hearted and bind up their wounds (Psalm 147:3 KJV). There is no correct way in which one heals. Healing is a process; it requires people to be open and honest about the feelings they feel from the hurt they have experienced. Healing can come in many different forms; one can seek counseling from their priest, a therapist or through prayer and meditation.

Heal me, O Lord, and I shall be healed; save me, and I shall be saved; you are my praise. (Jeremiah 17:14 KJV) Jeremiah the prophet, talks about how the people are praying to the Lord to heal their hearts.

It doesn't matter what kind of hurt it is God can heal, we have to believe and trust in him and his divine word, whether its physical or mental pain, whether it's an illness that take over our bodies, if we believe and have faith in God. God was wounded for our transgressions, he was bruised for our iniquities; the chastisement of our peace was upon him; and with stripes we are healed (Isaiah 53:5 KJV). How awesome is it that Jesus paid the ultimate price for us all. Take some time to think about the price he paid for our sins and for us to be free.

If your hurt is more physical than emotional there still lies a desire to be healed. God has the ability to heal anything Cancer, kidney failure, broken hearts, broken families to name a few. If you believe or have an ounce of faith you can experience the gift of healing.

"Is anyone among you sick? Let them call the elders of the church to pray over them and anoint them with oil in the name of the Lord". (James 5:14 NIV)

The following are scriptures that deal with the subject of healing.

James 5:13-14 (KJV; NIV)
Jeremiah 17:14 (KJV; NIV)
Isaiah 53:5 (KJV; NIV)
Jeremiah 6:14 (KJV; NIV)
Matthew 10:8 (KJV; NIV)
Faith James 5:15—16

U—Understanding

"Give me understanding and I shall keep thy Law" (Psalm 119:34; KJV).

It is important to understand that everyone will experience some form of hurt at some point in their life. Being aware of your feelings and what caused the hurt is a critical component to experiencing a healing. With knowledge and wisdom we will be better equipped to deal with hurt. God wants his people to have an understanding of his word and in all we do. God said "my people were destroyed because of lack of knowledge and wisdom".

The following are scriptures which deals with the subject of Understanding:

Hosea 4:6
Proverbs: 14:29

R—Restore

Restore means to put something back together again, to mend, to make it better or whole again. God can restore our hearts, minds, body, and the hurt we have experienced in life. God has the power to make everything new again. People have the power to restore old friendships, marriages, relationship with God or anything else that has been neglected in life

"Restore unto me the joy of your salvation; and uphold me with your spirit". (Psalm51:12KJV)

The following are scriptures that deal with the subject of Restoration:

Psalm 23:3
Deuteronomy 22:2
Jeremiah 27:22

T—Trust

Webster dictionary (2016) defines trust as the belief that someone or something is reliable, good, honest, and effective.

Often times when people experience hurt they are unable to trust others. Trust is something that takes a lot of work, trust is not developed over night it is a process like everything else in life. It is important to believe that we can overcome being hurt in life. We must trust God with our situation. "God is not a man, that he should lie; neither the son of man, that he should repent: hath he said, and shall he not do it? Or hath he spoken, and shall he not make it good? (Numbers 23:19; KJV).

"I can do all things through Christ who gives me strength" (KJV Philippians 4:13).

"Trust in the Lord with all hearts and lean not to our own understanding, in all ways acknowledge him, and he shall direct thy path" (Proverbs 3:5-6).

Psalm 37:4-5
Numbers 23:19
Psalm 37:1

I Trust You Lord!

I Trust You Lord

When I'm Lonely and Sad

I Trust You Lord

Through my trials and tribulations

I Trust You Lord

When I am Worried

I Trust You Lord

When I'm In Pain or my Heart has been wounded

And seems to cause me Hurt

I Trust You Lord

B.N.W.

H—Hope & Help

We must have hope. "May the God of hope fill you with all joy and peace as you trust in him, so that you may overflow with hope by the power of the Holy Spirit". (Romans 15:13 NIV) When we have expectations and a desire for something we have hope. When we wish for something or seek to accomplish a goal in life we must have faith that we can and will do what we have set out to do. The bible speaks about how God's will give us the desires of our heart (PSALM 37:4) Hope creates a feeling of expectation, it gives us a reason to live and love. Hope increases our confidence because we know with God all will be well.

"I lift up my eyes to the mountains, where does my help come from? My help comes from the Lord, the Maker of heaven and earth. (Psalm 121:1-2 KJV) God is our refuge and strength, a very present help in time of trouble (Psalm 46:1KJV; NIV) When we are in trouble our heavenly father help us, no matter what it is. He will give us favor in the court room with the judge, God gives us favor everyday with something or someone. He uses people to help us in certain situations, he use people in schools, hospitals, and he will send the right person to help us. God will put angels around us to help us. When we make the wrong the decisions or get ourselves in to situations that we should not be. Who's there? God is. God will never leave us nor forsake us. God is merciful, and his mercy is new every day.

The following are scriptures that help deal with the subject of hope and help.

Psalm 27:7-10
Psalm 46:1

U—Unity and Unconditional Love

Unity is when we can all come together and are on one accord and are in agreement with one another. Unity should exist on the job, in relationships, marriages, family, and in the church, God is pleased when we all work in unity, God does not like when people are unpleasant, inconsistent and not on one accord. God does not bless where there is dysfunction, God does not Bless mess.

Ephesians 4:13
1 Peter 3:8
1 Corinthians 10
Philippians 2:2

Unconditional Love is Godly love; God loves us all the same. His love is the same each and every day. We as parents love our children unconditionally no matter what. Unconditional Love is real; you see no size skinny or fat, dark or light skin, see no race, no color (black, white or brown), its simply unconditional love. God loves us all and he will be the one to decide on what is right and wrong, so do not judge anyone of their past or mistakes in life. God doesn't look at our past; we as believers are constantly trying to improve ourselves. The book of John tells us that there is no greater love than God's love and that he laid down his life for us,(John15:3 KJV) Now that's Love.

The following are scriptures that deal with the subject unconditional love.

Colossians 3:14
Ephesians 2:4–5

Unconditional love is garnered and shared by those who love themselves first. In Christianity, unconditional love is thought to be part of the Four Loves: affection, friendship, eros, and charity. In Psychology, unconditional love refers to a state of mind in which one has the goal of increasing the welfare of another, despite any evidence of benefit for oneself.

R—Respect

If we do not have respect for ourselves, we cannot respect others. We must treat others the way we want to be treated in life. Showing respect can also keep you from causing hurt to someone. Respect will make you think before you speak.

The following are scriptures which deal with the subject of respect.

Matthew 7:12
Philippians 2:3

T—Teach & Transform

Teach me o Lord the way of thy statues; and I shall keep it unto the end (PSALM 119:33).

To teach is to educate, you can teach someone with both good and bad experiences in life to help them overcome issues they may be dealing with. One person's mistake can help another person from making the same mistake. Christians believes that God's word will teach us all things once we have experienced a relationship with God (John 14:26KJV; Bible). Every day we all learn something new, we never truly stop learning.

The following are scriptures that deal with the subject of Teach.

Psalm 27:11
John 14:26
Luke 12:12
John 16:13
1 Corinthians 2:10

Transform

To transform is to change our appearance or character, we can also transform our hearts to be more loving and God like. We can transform our way of thinking from negative to positive. We can change our style of clothing that we wear, and our hair. In today's world many people find things they don't like about them psychically, for example people can have surgery to transform their bodies, eye sight, and hair loss. Anything can be changed for the right price. However transformation of the mind is the most powerful thing one can change. Transforming how we think, and view people can make the world a better place.

"And do not be conformed to this world, but be transformed by the renewing of your mind, so that you may prove what the will of God is, that which is good and acceptable and perfect". (Romans 12:2 KJV)

Create in me a clean heart O God, and renew a steadfast spirit within me (Psalm 51:10 NIV; KJV).

The following are scriptures that deal with the subject of transforming.

Ezekiel 36:26
Ezekiel 18:31
2 Corinthians 5:17
Titus 3:5
Colossians 1:21-22
Ephesians 4:22-24

Ways to Change

Renewing of our mind

Accepting Christ

Being Born Again

Testing our Faith, Love, Honesty, our heart, Forgiveness,

Love for one another

Cleansing the Body

Knowing the will of God

Thinking Thoughts of good and not evil

Show Kindness

Transforming our Hearts

HURT & HURT

When Love ones Leave
to go to that heavenly place
We HURT
When there is pain in our bodies
WE HURT
When unkind words are spoken
about us
WE HURT
When we do not feel Loved
WE HURT
But there's one place we will never
Hurt again, it is the
wonderful and amazing place
That God has prepared for us all;
Where we will never Hurt Again!

BNW

In Closing

I would like to thank you for taking the time to read this book. I pray whoever reads this book will be delivered and set free from all the hurt they have held on to in their life. I pray that you learn to forgive and move forward in life and Christ. I am grateful to God for giving me this opportunity to reach out to others.

About the Author

In 1990, I was licensed as an Evangelist by the late Bishop Henrietta Jones of God's Helping Hands Holy Temple, located in Los Angeles, California. Bishop Jones was a great mentor and always encouraged me to write a book to help others heal from their hurt. In 1995, I was ordained as an Elder by Dr. Dorothy and Bishop Dennis Evans of Refuge Christian Center, located in Pasadena, California. I thank God for sending me two amazing and powerful women to help me along the way.

Betty Attended University of Phoenix where she obtained an Associates of Psychology. She is a proud member of the National Society of Collegiate Scholars. She is married with four children and two grandchildren. She is a devoted Christian who truly loves the Lord.

In 2013, I had a dream, in the dream I was given the title Hurt & Hurt. I knew right then, I was to follow what God was revealing to me, to help others. I always wondered why I struggled with so much pain and then one day I realized it would be my testimony of how God healed and delivered me. The hurt I had experienced as a child and as an adult caused me to pray and trust in God. I surrounded myself with people I believed could provide me with the prayer and support I needed. I knew holding on to hurt would only cause me more pain and I was determined to be set free, so I decided to deal directly with the root of my hurt. My hurt began at an early age when my schoolmates would tease me about the color of my skin. I also experienced hurt from family and personal relationships. Once I realized the areas in my life in which I experienced the most hurt I began praying for deliverance morning, noon, and night. One day God answered my prayers and all my feelings of hurts were no longer, I felt free and restored in my spirt and life.

I pray these words of wisdom will be guidance to others.

To God Be the Glory!

Daily Activities

Write something Positive you did today.

_____

_____

_____

_____

_____

_____

_____

_____

_____

_____

_____

_____

_____

_____

_____

_____

_____

_____

_____

_____

_____

_____

_____

_____

_____

_____

_____

Daily Activities

Write down someone you have forgiven.

_____

_____

_____

_____

_____

_____

_____

_____

_____

_____

_____

_____

_____

_____

_____

_____

_____

_____

_____

_____

_____

_____

_____

_____

_____

Daily Activities

Pray and Ask God to place love in your heart for those who have caused you pain.

_____
_____
_____
_____
_____
_____
_____
_____
_____
_____
_____
_____
_____
_____
_____
_____
_____
_____
_____
_____
_____
_____
_____
_____
_____
_____

Daily Activities

Write down 3 steps you can take today to help you
overcome the hurt you feel.

_____

_____

_____

_____

_____

_____

_____

_____

_____

_____

_____

_____

_____

_____

_____

_____

_____

_____

_____

_____

_____

_____

_____

_____

_____

_____

_____

Daily Activities

Pray for guidance, strength and motivation.

_____
_____
_____
_____
_____
_____
_____
_____
_____
_____
_____
_____
_____
_____
_____
_____
_____
_____
_____
_____
_____
_____
_____
_____
_____
_____
_____
_____
_____

Notes:

Notes:

Notes:

_____
_____
_____
_____
_____
_____
_____
_____
_____
_____
_____
_____
_____
_____
_____
_____
_____
_____
_____
_____
_____
_____
_____
_____
_____
_____
_____
_____
_____
_____
_____

Notes:

Notes:

_____
_____
_____
_____
_____
_____
_____
_____
_____
_____
_____
_____
_____
_____
_____
_____
_____
_____
_____
_____
_____
_____
_____
_____
_____
_____
_____
_____
_____
_____
_____
_____
_____
_____

Notes:

_____
_____
_____
_____
_____
_____
_____
_____
_____
_____
_____
_____
_____
_____
_____
_____
_____
_____
_____
_____
_____
_____
_____
_____
_____
_____
_____
_____
_____
_____
_____
_____

Notes:

_____
_____
_____
_____
_____
_____
_____
_____
_____
_____
_____
_____
_____
_____
_____
_____
_____
_____
_____
_____
_____
_____
_____
_____
_____
_____
_____
_____
_____
_____
_____

Notes:

Notes:

_____

_____

_____

_____

_____

_____

_____

_____

_____

_____

_____

_____

_____

_____

_____

_____

_____

_____

_____

_____

_____

_____

_____

_____

_____

_____

_____

_____

_____

_____

Notes:

Challenges:

_____
_____
_____
_____
_____
_____
_____
_____
_____
_____
_____
_____
_____
_____
_____
_____
_____
_____
_____
_____
_____
_____
_____
_____
_____
_____
_____
_____
_____
_____
_____

Challenges:

_____
_____
_____
_____
_____
_____
_____
_____
_____
_____
_____
_____
_____
_____
_____
_____
_____
_____
_____
_____
_____
_____
_____
_____
_____
_____
_____
_____
_____
_____

Challenges:

_____
_____
_____
_____
_____
_____
_____
_____
_____
_____
_____
_____
_____
_____
_____
_____
_____
_____
_____
_____
_____
_____
_____
_____
_____
_____
_____
_____
_____
_____
_____
_____

Challenges:

_____

_____

_____

_____

_____

_____

_____

_____

_____

_____

_____

_____

_____

_____

_____

_____

_____

_____

_____

_____

_____

_____

_____

_____

_____

_____

_____

_____

_____

_____

_____

Challenges:

_____

_____

_____

_____

_____

_____

_____

_____

_____

_____

_____

_____

_____

_____

_____

_____

_____

_____

_____

_____

_____

_____

_____

_____

_____

_____

_____

_____

_____

_____

Challenges:

_____

_____

_____

_____

_____

_____

_____

_____

_____

_____

_____

_____

_____

_____

_____

_____

_____

_____

_____

_____

_____

_____

_____

_____

_____

_____

_____

Challenges:

_____
_____
_____
_____
_____
_____
_____
_____
_____
_____
_____
_____
_____
_____
_____
_____
_____
_____
_____
_____
_____
_____
_____
_____
_____
_____
_____
_____
_____

Challenges:

_____

_____

_____

_____

_____

_____

_____

_____

_____

_____

_____

_____

_____

_____

_____

_____

_____

_____

_____

_____

_____

_____

_____

_____

_____

_____

_____

Challenges:

_____

_____

_____

_____

_____

_____

_____

_____

_____

_____

_____

_____

_____

_____

_____

_____

_____

_____

_____

_____

_____

_____

_____

_____

_____

_____

_____

Challenges:

_____

_____

_____

_____

_____

_____

_____

_____

_____

_____

_____

_____

_____

_____

_____

_____

_____

_____

_____

_____

_____

_____

_____

_____

_____

_____

_____

_____

_____

End

Dedication

Dedication To The Master the Creator of all things, My Heavenly Father Whom I Trust and look to each and everyday.

God Bless!

Betty N. Waggoner

Printed in the United States
By Bookmasters